T0210001

ABOUT FACE

GETTING TO KNOW THE MEN BEHIND THE MONEY

Autumn Kirsch

WestBow Press books may be ordered through booksellers or by contacting:

WestBow Press
A Division of Thomas Nelson & Zondervan
1663 Liberty Drive
Bloomington, IN 47403
www.westbowpress.com
844-714-3454

ISBN: 978-1-6642-1836-9 (sc)
ISBN: 978-1-6642-1837-6 (e)

Print information available on the last page.

WestBow Press rev. date: 1/4/2021

WESTBOW
PRESS®
A DIVISION OF THOMAS NELSON
& ZONDERVAN

ABOUT FACE

GETTING TO KNOW THE MEN
BEHIND THE MONEY

If George Washington saw his face on the one-dollar bill, just how would he feel?

Looking back at his accomplished life, George
Would definitely remember the harsh winter at Valley Forge,
And how he bravely led his army corps
Against the British in the Revolutionary War.
He was the leader of the Continental Army, not to mention,
He led the Constitutional Convention.
In 1789 he became the nation's first president,
And to the Bill of Rights he did consent.
He signed a bill creating the Bank of the United States,
And he certainly would appreciate
The sight of his face on the one-dollar bill.

If Abraham Lincoln saw his face on the five-dollar bill, just how would he feel?

Would he laugh, would he cry?

Would he tip his stove-pipe hat and sigh?

He would remember back to 1834,

The years before the Civil War,

For during this time it did occur

That he served in the Illinois state legislature.

Lincoln would lament over the Civil War,

Over the deaths and divided nation to restore.

Though he might even smile, it's anyone's guess,

To think he affirmed the nation's "new birth of freedom" in the Gettysburg Address.

He felt that Americans had a moral obligation,
And he disagreed with the expansion of slavery in the Emancipation Proclamation.
Before the nation's Reconstruction did occur,
Lincoln was killed in a theatre,

But maybe if Lincoln was still alive,
He'd be surprised to see his face on the five... dollar bill.

If Alexander Hamilton saw his face on the ten-dollar bill, just how would he feel?
He might think back to the time when he was twenty-years-old,
He became George Washington's aide and Lieutenant Colonel, so brave and so bold.
He saw action at Trenton and Princeton in the military,
And then his career path turned toward Washington, D.C.
He wrote over half of the Federalist Papers, a powerful writer,
And favored strong central government, as a political insider.
His belief in government and his determination
Helped popularize the Constitution and its ratification.
Looking at his monetary face, Hamilton would clearly
Remember becoming the first Secretary of the Treasury.
Although killed in a duel to which he did concur
By a political opponent named Aaron Burr,

Hamilton would definitely be glad
To see the impact on America he had
And his face on the ten-dollar bill.

If Andrew Jackson saw his face on the twenty-dollar bill, just how would he feel?

He might think back to when he was 13, when he joined the Revolutionary War,

And how in 1812 he was ready to fight even more.

He would remember the famous Battle of New Orleans,

His life as the seventh president, and the years in between.

He was tough and gained "Old Hickory" as his nickname,

While Cherokee Indians felt he was to blame.

They were sent from the lands they had lived on for years

On a journey now known as the Trail of Tears.

He referred to himself as a common man,
And may find it strange to see his face span
The width of the twenty-dollar bill.

If Ulysses S. Grant saw his face on the fifty-dollar bill, just how would he feel?
He might first reflect on his youth and then agree
He gained valuable experience at West Point Army Academy.
He was commander of Union Army forces during the Civil War,
And helped the Union gain what it hoped for.
After winning battles at Vicksburg and Chattanooga in 1863,
A surrender was later offered by Robert E. Lee.
He became a war hero, and it was self-evident
He would serve as the nation's next president.
After leaving office, he traveled worldwide,

And would certainly feel quite dignified
To see his face on the fifty-dollar bill.

If Benjamin Franklin saw his face on the one-hundred-dollar bill, just how would he feel?
He might first remember back to when he was 12 years of age,
For it was then that he turned many a page.
He had a love for reading, whether it was summer or winter,
And he became an apprentice to his brother, a printer.
Young Franklin traveled to Philadelphia to find work at his trade,
And later began a printing business with the money he made.
He eventually purchased the *Pennsylvania Gazette*.
It became the most successful newspaper in the colonies, he would not forget.
He published *Poor Richard's Almanac* from which people learned,
"A penny saved is a penny earned."

After retiring and gaining self-reliance
He turned to the world of experimentation and science.
He invented bifocals, not to mention,
The Franklin stove was a most useful invention.
In the early 1750s, he studied electricity
With his famous experiment of the kite and the key.
In the Declaration of Independence and Constitution Franklin's signature can be found,
A hard worker, great thinker and American all-around.

All of his accomplishments and the life that he led
Are why his face is found on the one-hundred... dollar bill.

There's one type of bill we've yet to review.
Can you guess which it is? Yes, it's the two!
Thomas Jefferson's face is the one that appears,
And he achieved many milestones over the years.
He wrote the Declaration of Independence which affirmed God's gift of inalienable rights,
And then to political office he set his sights.
He served as governor of Virginia and then U.S. minister to France for a time,
And became the first Secretary of State in 1789.
He served as vice president for four years,
And in 1800 he began his presidential career.
He negotiated the Louisiana Purchase in 1803,
Furthering our country's expansion toward Manifest Destiny.

All of this and more Jefferson accomplished, it's true,
And he'd be proud to see his face on the two... dollar bill.

All of these men proudly served our nation.
They contributed many ideas and participated with great dedication.
So next time you take out your money, if you will,
Take note of the face on the green-colored bill!

ABOUT THE AUTHOR

Autumn Kirsch is a wife and mother of one son. She has a passion for learning – especially learning from the past – which fuels her interest in US and world history. Autumn graduated from Texas A&M University-Corpus Christi with a bachelor's degree in communication and from Columbia Southern University with an MBA. Autumn has made a career out of helping leaders and teams make successful organizational transitions in times of great change. Her hobbies include studying, antiquing with her husband and looking for dinosaur bones with her son in her great home state of Texas.

Printed in the United States
By Bookmasters